Buyer's Remorse

Buyer's Remorse

Poems by Roy Mash

For Maria,
Thanks for your support
& Friendship,

Roy

Cherry Grove Collections

ISBN: 9781625490513
LCCN: 2013952187

Published by Cherry Grove Collections

Poetry Editor: Kevin Walzer

Business Editor: Lori Jareo

P.O. Box 541106

Cincinnati, OH 45254-1106

www.cherry-grove.com

Book jacket design by Jeremy Thornton, www.jftdesign.com

Cover art and doodles by Roy Mash

for Kathy and Adam

Acknowledgments

I wish to thank the editors of the following journals in which these poems first appeared:

14 by 14: "We Here"
99 Poems for the 99 Percent: "Press Conference"
Agni Online: "Graph Paper"
Ambush Review: "&," "Umlaut"
Atlanta Review: "Buyer's Remorse," "Glasses," "Intimations of Mortality,, "The Untouchables"
Avatar Review: "Dentist Chair," "Sky Mall," "X-Ray Vision"
Barrow Street: "The Incredible Shrinking Man"
California Quarterly Review: "Anti-Aubade," "On Taking Criticism"
The Dirty Napkin: "Tall Man"
DMQ Review: "Creature from the Black Lagoon"
The Evansville Review: "Whenever I See Her," "A Plate of Scrambled Eggs"
Larkfield Review: "The Plagiarizer of Words"
Marin Poetry Center Anthology: "Tuesday"
Miller's Pond: "Pinkie," "Thumb," "Index," "Stomach"
Nimrod: "Pants", "Knee as Nostalgia"
The Paterson Literary Review: "Making the Bed", "The Worst Way to Go", "Long Division"
Passages North: "Letter to My Penis"
Poetry Midwest: "Doodle"
Poetry East: "Cannonball", "The Nature of the Cartoon", "You and I"
Prick of the Spindle: "Neckroll"
Rhino: "'They'll Never Find Me Here'"
River Styx: "Two Saints of Clarity", "Wallet"
Serving House Journal: "Desire for Retirement", "The Formalist Flattered", "Synopsis"
The Sow's Ear: "The Ankle in the Café," "Hardly Lord Jim"
Spillway: "The Day I Found I Could Count Forever". "Shock", "Cuticle"
The Road Not Taken: "Backache," "Love of Slapstick"
Two Review: "Cartwheels"
West Marin Review: "I Was Getting Ready To Tie My Tie When"

"Press Conference" was anthologized in *99 Poems for the 99 Percent*, ed. Dean Rader, 2013.
"The Worst Way to Go" was reprinted in *Marin Poetry Center Anthology*, ed. Rose Black.
"Pinkie," "Thumb," "Index," and "Cartwheels" were reprinted in *Larkfield Review*.
"Doodle" and "Intimations of Mortality" were anthologized in *The Well of Living Waters*, ed. Lenore Weiss, 2012.
"The Incredible Shrinking Man" was reprinted in *phati'tude*.
"Cartwheels" was awarded second place in the 2008 *Two Review* Poetry Contest.
"Glasses", "Mt. Tamalpais", and "The Untouchables" received International Publication Prizes from *Atlanta Review*.

Contents

Introduction

I

Glasses	3
Wallet	4
Mt. Tamalpais	6
The Day I Found I Could Count Forever	7
Cartwheels	8
Cannonball	10
The Incredible Shrinking Man	12
Intimations of Mortality	14
Creature from the Black Lagoon	15
The Untouchables	16
The Nature of the Cartoon	18
X-Ray Vision	20
Hardly Lord Jim	21
The Worst Way to Go	22
"They'll Never Find Me Here"	24

II

Love of Slapstick	27
Doodle	28
Sky Mall	30
Buyer's Remorse	32
Synopsis	33
Press Conference	34
Cuticle	35
Making the Bed	36
Tuesday	37
Pants	38
Live Action X-Ray	40
The Ankle in the Café	42
Sneeze	44
Dentist Chair	46

III

Shock	49
Couple Snoring	49
I Was Getting Ready to Tie My Tie When	49
Mate	50
Desire for Retirement	51
Backache	52
Neck Roll	54
Knee as Nostalgia	55
Anti-Aubade	56
You and I	57
Whenever I See Her	58
Letter to My Penis	60

IV

Pinkie	65
Thumb	67
Index	68
Tall Man	70
A Plate of Scrambled Eggs	73
Stomach	74
On Taking Criticism	76
The Formalist Flattered	77
The Plagiarizer of Words	78
Umlaut	79
&	80
Two Saints of Clarity	81
Long Division	82
We Here	83
Graph Paper	84
The Mark of Zorro	85

Introduction

Robert Frost was once asked, "What do you look for when you pick up a book by another poet?" Frost replied, "I look for how the poet takes himself and how he takes his subject." And, yes, I'm old enough to have been present for the exchange. Frost went on to make clear that "how a poet takes himself and how he takes his subject" has to do with tone, the author's "implicit attitude toward the reader and the people, places and events in a work."

Roy Mash is an original. Well-read in contemporary poetry, he has a style, a tone, an approach all his own. The poems are, by turns, serious, happy, brooding, and jauntily playful. He respects his reader, and brings to the poems a respect for and dedication to the craft.

At the same time there's a joking, a sometimes jocular delight in language. I think of W. H. Auden and that remark of his, "A poet is, before anything else, a person who is passionately in love with language." He may not be exactly what Auden envisioned, but Roy Mash is a shrewd practitioner of the art, a man playfully and passionately in love with language:

> Come, spritz of seltzer in the face,
> implacable banana peel.
> Come, brickbats, pratfalls, amazing grace-
> lessness, the yowl of the schlemiel.
>   [from "Love of Slapstick"]

And what of the title? Why *Buyer's Remorse*? The title works. Still there's certain darkness to the word *remorse*. A number of the poems—on first reading—seem "easy," poems of skill and a particular panache, poems of "spirited style." These include "Umlaut," "Graph Paper," and "The Plagiarizer of Words," whose title character

. . . snitches words like a frog snatching flies:
thimble   haphazard   numbskull
which collage themselves like Rockettes which
sets him off on:
collision   kalashnikov
the syllables wiggling and kicking in his mouth . . .

I sometimes think of poem and book titles as "ways into," as clues, if indeed clues are needed, to the author's particular slant on the world, the workings of his mind and his intention. So it was I asked Roy Mash, "What led you to choose that particular title for the book?" I think it works. No problem. I'm just curious. There's a certain "darkness" to the word itself, yet—in my mind—the book is not particularly dark. On the contrary, I find it possessing a seemingly carefree sparkle, particularly in poems like "Wallet," "Glasses" and "Cartwheels."

Roy says he chose the title precisely because of the undertone of darkness in this otherwise breezy phrase. And it's true: On closer reading the humor in the book is often tinged with a dark underside. In the title poem, for example, there is the idea of ultimate dissatisfaction with one's own life; in "Making the Bed" we find the sense of false promise; "Sky Mall," "Dentist Chair," and "Intimations of Mortality" deal with fear; "A Plate of Scrambled Eggs" and "Creature From the Black Lagoon" treat sexuality and violence, or better, the sexuality of violence.

Buyer's Remorse is at once accessible, seemingly transparent and yet satisfying and rewarding to readers—and I imagine there are many—who will want to return to these poems again and again.

— Robert Sward, Santa Cruz, CA

I

Glasses

All day they've ridden me
along the trails
of the city, down one gully

and up another, digging
their heels
into the sides of my nose,

patting my plodding
head and whispering encouragement
into my ears.

Now, dismounted onto
the nightstand,
folded back into their old

lotus position, they've let
the moonlight pass through them
its two pools of silver,

while I graze nearby,
unsaddled
in the fuzzy tumbleweed.

They know
I will not wander far.

Wallet

for J. M.

Little papoose
   riding in my back pocket,
little clam, little pal,
   I love the tug
of you—
   pale imprint
of who I am,
   calm pull
of the always there.

■

Or is it me
   that's the papoose? You—
the dad
   who always pays
for dinner,
   the one
I never need to thank
   or ever think
twice about.

■

This morning I panicked
   again, finger-diving
every crease in the couch
   while you—
you just sat there
   on top of the dresser
where I'd left you
   last night
with a mental note.

■

I pity women
   with their purses
like canyons.
   I pity you—
reincarnated there,
   a chartreuse thing
with a fat snap,
   lost in the commotion of keys,
lipstick, Kleenex, pennies.

     ■

Little loner, you—
   little black
paladin of identity,
   how deftly
the twenties slide
   into place,
weathered lovers
   edging
into a leathered bed.

     ■

Ah, here's the ferry now.
   I reach back
with my finger and thumb,
   gesture
reflexive as breath,
   to lift you—
softwing, wornskin—
   one more time
into the hard world.

Mt. Tamalpais

I should be content
to look at a mountain
for what it is
and not as a comment
on my life.
　　　　　— David Ignatow

Its slopes are drawn into an unmistakable frown,
expressive of its disappointment with my lack
of grandeur, my raggy pup tent of a life.
The redwoods, swayed to its opinion,
are making the finger motion for shame.
Every day I drive by, a mote on my way to work,
there it is, clucking its tongue, red-penciling my thoughts
as they go by: lame . . . lame . . . triple X . . . lame.

Years from now, leaving the movie of my life,
it turns to its wife to compare notes.
"Eh," they agree, exchanging majestic shrugs,
"Two stars. Uneven pacing. Miscast. No arc."
Though they did like the part where I got hepatitis
in Greece, mostly for the cinematography.

The Day I Found I Could Count Forever

I was standing on the bed.
My mother
was pulling up my underpants.

She must have been weary
of my parade
of what-comes-next questions.

At each stop — A Hundred! A Thousand! –
a white door
would magically appear

just as the room was darkening
with nines,
those great elephants.

As the last one clomped into place,
the door would open
into a fresh room, empty and golden,

incomparably bigger, which my mind
began to fill
until it too brimmed with nines.

Then I understood:
There must be another, even bigger room beyond.
But then . . . But then . . . Oh . . .   Oh . . .

O . . .

Cartwheels

Young girls reeled them off
with such ease and delight.

It was all pinwheels
and spindrift, windmills

and giggle fits, dropped
coins that roll

with grace. Mine
of course were all buck

and bungle, botched
comical affairs, not unlike

early attempts at flight:
the nose plow,

the rump suddenly
prominent, the droll

implosion into a trough.
Rubber bands hitched

the propellers of my
legs to the wrapped

ball of my heart, not
a pretty sight.

Fifty years on,
there's no question

of getting it right, no postponed
redemption for the klutz.

Summer's mayhem,
for all its charms,

rolls off my rickety back.
Grace is now

an afternoon nap
as the drapes sashay

in their quiet orbits,
and the fan's shadow

blades ease
into their backstroke,

and blood performs
its clunky round

through fingertips and toes,
and somewhere is

the sound of spokes
ticking to a stop.

Cannonball

It was a great *pow* of a dive,
made for boys who specialized in feats of little skill
　　and spectacular effect;

　　impudent competition
for the God-shaped swan, all breast and feather
　　and grace, the jackknife

　　that released itself
to slit the water like a lover's hand slipping
　　into an open robe.

　　What was elegance
but a thing to be expunged, undone
　　by the effrontery

　　of a nice fat splurge,
the gaudy broadside of an éclair shrapneling the cheeks
　　of chubby summer.

　　Goodbye, cruel world!
the wrecking ball of the body cymbal-crashed
　　into the smug surface,

　　depth charge churning
in a blue fury of bubbles, cool nucleus of boy
　　sizzling in the silent below.

Was ever anything
more splendiferous than the sheer, stupid pleasure
of making a mess?

To geyser up like truth, starshot
across a world smithereened with watery rubble
and the shrieks of

poolside girls dismayed
by the brash, flamboyant, uncontainable *kaboom* of
You! You! You!

The Incredible Shrinking Man

For The Incredible Shrinking Man
every particle of dust was a monument
to his insignificance, an article
not of faith, but reverse magnificence.

First the phone handle dwarfed
his face. Then his belt ran out of holes.
Inside a month he morphed into such
as the finest whisker could not tickle.

What could it betoken that the kitten
was a monster out to kill
him? The spider was no joke either,
hairy and humongous, daintily

tiptoeing across the broad veldt
of the basement. Even as he drove
the sword of a pin intrepidly
through its innards, he knew

it was the close-up of the pincers,
and the maw, moist behind them,
that would stick with him. In the end
he got religion. Striding through

the screen whose once fine mesh
now formed portals several times
his height, he saw God saw all,
no matter how small. A lame conclusion

to a great premise. What happened next
the movie never said. Did he fall
through the floor of the ground?
Ride gigantic gossamers above?

How could he breathe when
an atom of oxygen outweighed
him? What would he see
when he grew tinier than light?

Civilizations an angstrom wide
where he might pause to fall
in love before he fell through
them, too? I like to think he finally

resolved himself to falling,
to make a life of falling
down through the sweet infinite
divisibility of oblivion.

Intimations of Mortality

As a boy I imagined Karloff's Mummy
set off from Egypt, plodding dunes,
arms ever out in the usual Mummy way,
on his mission to Detroit, and me.

Now and again I plot him across the years,
stilting in black and white along the long
Atlantic floor. No character development here,
yet each . . . dumb . . . effortful . . . step: a progression.

Rarely as a rule do I dwell on the horror.
Cursed and carefree as any archeologist,
I bustle about, running errands, playing ball;
me so nimble, and him so far.

How slow the director had him project
his shadow . . . across . . . the screen.
Only my buddy's wisecrack cut
the fear, helped me make it through to the end:

Anybody who gets caught by The Mummy
deserves to die!

Creature from the Black Lagoon

In the poster he carries the fainted
heroine, bridegroom style in his scaly arms,
like so much pliant linen, back into
the swamp, into the murk, into his lair.
Her arms are splayed, her neck slung back in lush
surrender, her breasts ascendant. He slogs
with flippered walk, goggle eyes swiveling
over the smorgasbord of her torso,
the bobbing calves, the hanging hair, all that
tainted helplessness. Later she will wake,
confused at first, then bring the back of her
hand to her open mouth to milk for us
the stark, unspeakable eternity
between the realization and the scream.

The Untouchables

I wanted to be 1932,
the spinning headlines,
the boy who hawked them,
the blood on the barbershop floor.

I wanted to be the contract
put out on Bugs or Lucky or Knuckles,
the hit men imported from Philly,
the snub-nose .38 special with the taped butt.

I wanted to be the filed-off serial number,
the East River,
Winchell's voiceover—staccato,
like a typewriter got caught in his throat.

I wanted to be the man in the fedora jumping
onto the running board
of the black-fendered Hudson
as it came squealing around the corner
detonating puddle after puddle,
the tommy guns flashing over their black bibs.

I wanted to be the shiny shoulder holsters
of the feds who couldn't be bought
or scared off, the statuette
of the phone Ness barked into,
the black bell of the earpiece
he held in two nonchalant fingers,
the star witness who defied the mob
and never made it to the stand.

I wanted to have just gotten sprung
from Sing Sing or Leavenworth by a slick mouthpiece,
to waltz into some joint
in a double-breasted pinstripe and spats,
with a moll on each elbow.
I wanted to *be* the molls.

Then Prohibition, like middle school, ended.
Jake Guzik, the bookkeeper, broke down, whining,
"Listen to me, Roy. We gotta go legit.
I'm tellin' ya. The old days are gone, Roy.
We gotta go legit."

I had to slap the worm around.
Nobody—not Jake,
not Johnny Fortunato,
not even Frank "The Enforcer" Nitti—
was going to keep me
from being
the dead fish left in the stoolie's postbox,
the slot in the door of the speakeasy,
the ringside smoke.

The Nature of the Cartoon

Some colorful creature
is always getting the better, or being got
the better of.

A canary with an oversized mallet
bops a cat,
whose body goes stiff and resonates like a gong.

A coyote ties himself to a rocket,
which cartwheels
all the way to outer space before

turning to scream straight down,
red veins
zig-zagging through his eyeballs.

The Master of the House, who seems to exist
wholly from the waist
down, sticks his toe into a socket.

His bright yellow skeleton
flashes like a marquee
above the checkered linoleum.

Not to worry!
Nothing lasts for long.
The hole

that appears in the belly
of the bear after he's been blasted with a shotgun
seals up in a moment, and he's jolly.

The steamroller may leave the duck
tottering and two-dimensional, but soon
he re-inflates and is good to go.

Nowhere will you find a zebra
lugged by its neck
from a watering hole, or larvae busy

emulsifying the soft tissue of a white caterpillar,
or your own liver
grown dull and hard and brown.

Happily, it is in the nature of the cartoon
for Charlie Darwin
to brain himself with a frying pan

until his eyes are drawn as X's,
and his tongue flops
like a pink rag out of the side of his mouth,

and the Grand Canyon telescopes below
as he steps
out onto the solid air.

X-Ray Vision

As a boy I wished for X-ray vision,
like Superman
but without his scruples.

You'd think one blouse layer
would be a snap for pupils
keen enough to bore through mountain,

child's play to pass
through a puny stratum of cashmere;
but it took practice,

I found, and precision,
to lay bare
with the delicate scalpels

of desire
the lurid cameo
in a comic book bubble

of dashes. Geezers now,
my eyes
without compunction

or ado
drill right through to the adorable
skeleton.

Hardly Lord Jim

I was the one
who got on all fours
behind chubby
and unsuspecting Fred
when Mike
shoved him in the chest
and he fell backward
over me
while Donny laughed.

That was it, as I remember.
Nobody went to the hospital.
There was no blood.
The grass
absorbed the fall,
most likely.

So
here I am
at the other end
of my life,
hardly Lord Jim,
but still
unable to put out
of my mind
me there
on all fours.

The Worst Way to Go

A perennial boyhood debate.

Of course it wasn't any good
    if you didn't imagine it
happening to you:

Burned alive. Buried alive. Eaten alive.
    (It was important to put in the part
about being alive.)

Hanging-drawing-and-quartering didn't seem
    so bad, until someone explained
the details. Then there was quicksand:

forced to breathe in goop in the dark alone,
    companions standing around
the smooth surface, alive.

In *Tarzan* they would string
    upside down some poor
native sap, never closely

identified, to the tips
    of two tall trees bent
to the ground for the purpose

of making a wishbone
    of him. The scream came
off-camera. It was pretty

quick, and you would think,
    Not so bad. Still, it could give you
the willies. For the rules said:

it had to be *you* strapped up there,
    you spraddled, you wriggling, you
waiting for the snap.

"They'll Never Find Me Here"

A paragraph, half-paragraph really,
tucked back with the local items. Some boy,
some other clever boy, somebody no-
body knew, someone certainly not me.

None of which ever stopped me from thinking
myself into the fridge in the far lot
down by the rusted-out pier, or making
my way back—back before the reek of shit,

back before the *Stupid! Stupid! Stupid!*,
before the kicking, the keening, the crazed
calling out, back before the black surround
and the seal like a kiss, before its sound,

to that instant of whispered glee, that one
heart surge of delight and exultation.

II

Love of Slapstick

Come, spritz of seltzer in the face,
implacable banana peel.
Come, brickbats, pratfalls, amazing grace-
lessness, the yowl of the schlemiel.

Away with wit, you clever flights
of phrase it takes a Ph.D.
to explicate. One good food fight's
worth fifty Oscar Wildes to me.

A can of paint on Keaton's head,
another on his foot: What bliss,
God bless the doofuses who spread
the net he manages to miss.

Come, whoopee cushions, slamming doors.
Come, bops and jabs and spit-takes sprayed
on brides by grooms with falling drawers,
O heaven of the seventh grade!

No sadism this, no black desire,
just Larry, Moe, and Curly's woes,
the thousand gouges that conspire
to make the milk come out my nose.

Come, O pie-faced end: my feet glued
to the floor, my tie caught in the gears,
the audience in stitches who
can't help but laugh themselves to tears.

Doodle

The hand begins by going off
on its own,
dashing across open space,
veering this way and suddenly that:
a pleasant careen,
the brain stuck in the backseat
staring out the window,
the pencil just along for the ride.

Feel of the page
on the side of the palm. Feel
of the pencil tip trailing
a wake of paper.
Feel of the freeeeway,
top down.
The skater's gracious embrace
of air.

It is as though the hand has eloped
with itself,
toddled off to trespass the blue
rules, the white divides:
a Ouija slider released from its ghost,
ambling among the portentous
letters and numbers and signs, happy
just to gibberish.

No one is watching. Nobody cares
if you are fool enough
to leave corkscrews all over the place, or if
in the mishmash of crisscross and curlicue,
something that looks like "Kathy"
should sprout like a Roman candle out of the top
of something
that might be a head.

Sky Mall

Now that the air has become a pavement
of potholes, the fuselage a chew toy
for the gods,
now that the wings have begun to flap
like a real bird's,
the peanuts bubbling out of the cup,
never before have I so wanted these things:
an upside-down tomato garden,
a scale that shows the time in Tokyo,
a wall-size *NY Times* crossword puzzle.

Somewhere a baby is bawling annoyingly
inside me. When the flight attendants are asked
to take their seats,
I am surprised I have lived this long
without a Frankenstein bobblehead,
an inflatable electric piano,
a precise-portion pet feeder.

The descent is too steep, too steep!
I must have these night vision binoculars,
the talking Spanish-English dictionary,
the collection of Lincoln pennies
with the rare 1943 steel cent.

I play the game of closing my eyes,
testing each moment for the soothing jolt
that signals the end.

Will it never come?

I want to go home,
to sit at my desk with the Boston Red Sox
laser-engraved paper weight
containing actual dirt from Fenway Park,
to fritter the afternoon on rounds
of touch-screen Texas Hold'em,
to drift off in flannel
footed pajamas,
as a beige belt
sends gentle, slimming current
to my midriff.

Buyer's Remorse

Even before the gull-doored DeLorean pulls out
of the lot, before the best man launches
into his bawdy toast, before the ink has dried
on the time-share in Tahiti, before
the French fries that smelled so comforting
begin to roil once again in the wire basket
of your belly, somewhere near the back
of your skull a tiny tuning fork is keening:
Mistake! Mistake! Mistake!

But by this time you've accepted the post
in Borneo and are boarding the plane.
Your sweat has already baptized the hand-crafted,
bone-coffin cowboy boots that felt
practically custom-made when you rode them
up and down the glassy aisles of Louis Vuitton.
The six-volume set of Hume's *History of England*
stares reproachfully down from the topmost shelf,
its pages uncut, pristine as the Chopin *Étude*
on the programmable baby grand whose carcass
is parked in the center of your geodesic home.

This is the time for grieving, for getting ready
for the funeral, your life laid out on the bed
like some suede suit your wife warned you against.
You'd give it back if you could, but you've made
your choice and—hard luck—the outlet takes no returns.

Synopsis

Shelley's famous
diss shows
Ozymandias hapless
as dust
his ruckus
past his
bust bust

headless heedless
sans hands
sand's face
he's ghost
he's toast

he's
us

Press Conference

Actually
I
factually
lie,
but
so
what?
No

WMD?
Nay!
Bah!
Reality
c'est
moi.

Cuticle

Beneath
notice
this
swath,
thin
wave
of
skin,

poured
here
onto
the
hard
shore.

Making the Bed

There's a moment after the sheet's
been snapped,
cast into a bosomy sky
before it lapses in a shambles
at your knees,
when it seems as if it's going to amble
perfectly, consolingly
down,
like a hand
on a troubled shoulder,
a fatherly hand
that grows gentler, featherier
with nearness, promising
falsely,
"Everything's okay. Everything's
okay."

Tuesday

In mid-bite, the way
   the body
of the muffin suddenly crumbles,
   the palm frantic,
juggling the fragments.

The way you may feel your life
   come apart,
say on a Tuesday,
   feel it buckle,
then crumple . . .

The sick avalanche of surprise.

Pants

How inhuman they appear
this moment,
their loony ductwork rising to the illogical crotch,
the absurd absurd plurality of them.

The inseam alone is an abomination,
the zipper rippling, millipedal. Impossible
to believe anyone
ever ever cooked such things up.

Take the yodel,
or the Elizabethan ruff accordioned about a courtier's neck
like a poodle cut.
Oddities no more preposterous than this platypus

of apparel, emerging
just now
from the primordial soup of the clothes pile
onto the stark surface of awareness.

For two full minutes I *tsk* at the creation
of the belt loop, the undeserved
demise of the toga,
the singular goofiness of cuffs.

λ

And we who go into them,
feet first
each morning, sitting on the edge of the bed,
or stooped

to ladle the paraphernalia
of our sexes into the bladderchamber dangling
just there
about the shins,

we who furrow
our legs into their legs,
fork ourselves over to their keeping
down to the last follicle,

are we not, too,
silly silly creatures proliferating in our corduroys,
swaddled and monstrous and
perfectly crazy for the cha-cha.

Live Action X-Ray

Ghost food
   going down a ghost throat,
a sluice of grainy clots—

Gad the tongue's an ugly slug,
   glugging
in its cave—translucent sludge

like some gruel of souls
   poured over the gorge, draining down
into the hell

of the stomach,
   like something out of Bosch—
but without the color.

The Adam's apple,
   that horrible bobber,
that gobbler—

its undulations are enough
   to make you want to heave
and go on heaving

until there's nothing left
   to heave,
nothing left of you, until—

one day you get the knack
   of it, the trick
of transforming everyone

you see into a phantom,
    as though the sun'd become
an X-ray machine

and everyone on the street
    or in the café or at the beach:
just so much

walking rot,
    all their mortal yuckiness
on show, yet—

strangely alluring
    too,
skins thinned

to a kind of
    meshy chiffon,
all these lives

shawled in evanescence,
    and you feel
yourself enthralled

by the sheen of
    lusciousness—
feel your own lovely saliva

rising from the shadowy
    muck, shining
in the black glow.

The Ankle in the Café

dangles from a slanted knee
  beneath the table
kitty-corner from where I'm at
  bobbing as on
a tiny trampoline
  saluting
with each methodical throb
  the flag of yet
another unflappable day.
  The masterpiece of history
I've brought to read
  cannot compete
with the rise and fall
  of this feeble catapult
that lobs enchantment
  with each sway. When
    a slight
  arrhythmia jogs
        into a jiggle
              then breaks
      into full
  tilt until
      it has become a creature
unable to contain
              itself
  a thing let loose, unhinged

                         frenzied marlin on the   line
my dog Watson
                    who wags
       his whole behind
                              a wobbly baton
            flung
                         higgledy-piggledy
into the sky
                 the once   hypnotic
metronome
       now cracked and thrashing when
for no reason
   it simmers down
to coil itself
   about the other calf
charming as a barber pole.
   Even after
the owner has walked
   it out the door
and down the street
   something stays
beneath the table
   kitty-corner
patient and penned
     fibrillating.

Sneeze

and always this
   pretense
      toward still life
   the half-pant
backward
   the upbeat's raised
      baton poised
   on the instep
of breath
   the mortal
      coil and all
   its furious
potential

what agony
   were it
      to go on
   this little incision
in time
   where the last
      thing one wants
   is to
Be Here Now
   pinned
      to a tip
   a tiny
hyphen mosquitoed
   high up in the sky
      of the nostril
   whining
its poignance

the quizzical instant
   seized up
      like a suspender
   every last synapse
begging to be
   leapt
      to end
   this preposterous
syncopation
   to feel the body
      finally
lurch

that sweet apocalyptic
   smack
      of the catcher
   catching
the ball

Dentist Chair

I imagine I'm on a chaise lounge beside the pool, with my Mai Tai and my Ray-Bans and my belly that will not soon again be flat, ankles crossed in debonair repose. I like 4 pm, the way it smoothes itself over the wallpaper, its sheen of affable complacency like a captionless *New Yorker* cartoon.

The paper pillow, the blue bib clipped about my neck, are terribly reassuring. Mr. Insouciance, that's me! Turn a knob and it's Guantanamo, but here in temperature-controlled Room Number Two there is not permitted the least crumb of pain. Here is only cosseting; cosseting and concern for every twinge. "Did that hurt? No?" I reply in a telepathic vowel-only language, the Esperanto of dentistry.

Novocaine has turned two gums to girders and the nitrous has begun to sing. The slave trade, I read this morning, is booming. I open the hood of my face. What was it I was supposed to pick up at the store? Dr. Bloom and the hygienist peer in as at an old jalopy. Milk. . . . And what else? "Turn your head just a bit." What a great patient. So compliant. And such a dedicated flosser.

The mirror's pole has pulled back the slick sidewall of my cheek and shoved the rumpled tongue down and to the side. Carnage everywhere. That earthquake in China was horrible, horrible to think about. But hey, no tsunamis for me! The puddle of saliva at the back of my throat makes a popping, staticky sound snorkeling up the suction tube, something like *shchshchshchshch*, through which their shop talk—all mesial-this and buccal-that—dials in and out behind the modulated keening of the drill.

Sometimes it feels like I've spent half my life in this chair, here where there is always and only: Mouth. Mouth. Mouth. Mouth. My little mocker of the sky, little firmament in reverse. Sinkhole. Cul de sac. Old kit bag. Gob of my charmed days. I mumble something through the hardware and the cotton logs—something pithy, miraculous, oracular. "Spit," he says. And I spit.

III

Shock

the first time someone
　　called me "Sir" I looked around—
nobody was there

Couple Snoring

　　jackhammers battling
　　　　in the middle of the night—
　　no one to complain

I Was Getting Ready to Tie My Tie When

this kiss comes in time
　　stumbling on me as I am
standing in one sock

Mate

I want a woman who can play the Benoni blindfolded,
a woman whose deft Sicilian deflects
my frontal assault, a woman who knows

how to dominate the long diagonal,
her dark bishop
laying siege to my little house of pawns.

I want a woman
who has mastered the pin and the fork,
en passant and fianchetto,

a woman sharp, precocious,
with lofty degrees
and logical nostrils, a woman with ink stains

on the pockets of her shirt,
one who will take a chance on the Budapest Defense
when I am white.

My fingertips meet and bounce,
bounce and meet. She has been waiting three hours
for me to move.

Later I get down
the Greatest Games of Capablanca.
She removes her pince-nez,

and we go back over the variations
of the Ruy Lopez,
the Caro-Kann, the Giuoco Piano.

Desire for Retirement

Sometimes I envy my bed, how it gets to bask all day with the dog,
the pair of them loafing on the quiet raft of the afternoon,

lulled in the lapping of the clock, the still life still on the wall,
linens adrift on the shelf, the whole house awash with cushiness.

What is the work of the bed, but to bask all day with the dog?
What is the work of the dog, but to quiver his ear at the phone?

Somewhere is a midday world of penny loafers and bargain matinees,
saunas and marinas and ten-speeds and laptops in strudel cafés.

Bored? Me? Not. My plan's to saw off one day from the next,
to produce my quota of carbon dioxide, to throw myself into the job

of dabbing up the seeds that have fallen from an everything bagel
(though, to be truthful, I may delegate this to my little finger),

to join the road gang of sleepers-in, pay my dues to Local 6
of the lookers-out-of-windows, bow to the whims of my new boss

the *TV Guide*, take on the grunt work of doing zip; then every afternoon
at four, following my meeting with the Committee of Clouds,

to return, exhausted from a long day of breathing in and out,
to the bed and the dog, and tilt the glider of my nose

ever so slightly down, the descent so easeful, so gradual,
I won't even know when I'm on the ground.

Backache

1.

Waltzing in the wonder of why we're here.
What with the ice pack, the pillow under
my knees, the bathroom door like Everest
beckoning—far, near, far, near—the lyric
recurs consolingly. On the TV
of memory Fred is meandering
across the ceiling, and I am Ginger
full of grace, twirling backwards and in heels.

Though one budge and it's like a tennis ball
has been driven into a chain link fence,
a lumbar bulge that focuses my mind
(as the saying goes) *wonderfully*. Why
are we here? What keeps these voluptuous
W's dancing in the dark of my head?

2.

These days it no longer takes a couch lugged
upstairs, bullied through a doorway, nor sacks
of dry cement, nor an overhead smash,
nor Sundays sold into the servitude
of weeding. These days the teensiest twist
of the neck is enough. Seeing someone
one thought one knew, but didn't. The certain
belief in a nonexistent stair. Once

I was actually tearing off a bit
of Scotch tape (I swear!) when the voodoo stuck
its white surprise into the small of me,
and the universe collapsed to the head
of an angelic pin, and the pain spilled
out, and the floor became my only friend.

3.

That there was once a time I was able
to put on my own socks, it hurts to think.
Now every movement is a punishment.
Surely, I think, this must be how it is
with the gods, plastered to their mattresses
of hard cloud, ambulatory no more,
pumped up on anti-inflammatories,
so unsupple, so helpless to help us.

The ceiling, now Fredless, has relinquished
its fascination to the window drips,
which tango down the ballroom of the pane
sexily, their twining thighs streamed beneath
a mirrored globe. Look: there are two that bend
to kiss 'til the tune ends. And it soon ends.

Neck Roll

I'm scouring a little cylinder of air,
   turning the doorknob
of a body
   that gives
and groans and gives
   again. Hello head,
you sad horse.
   Aren't you tired
of your tether and the millstone
   of days, the bone
that grates inside each crick,
   each counter-crick? Wait
another few turns,
   then oh you gyring bird,
you loosey-goosey thing you,
   wheeler of walls
and ceilings and walls
   and floors and back again.
A few turns more,
   I imagine you rolling
right off, tumbling
   down the street,
happy to have at last
   unscrewed the sky
and left me here, a lost
   and Royless thing,
yet somehow happy too,
   limber, lolling
with the easy air
   of one who's cast
his only die.

Knee as Nostalgia

As history, it is a sad horse
in a sad pasture nibbling the sad sugar
from the palm of years gone by.

As diplomat, middleman, lugubrious. True
the decades merge, engage, but always with the same outcome.
The knee was made to bend in one direction only.

As old ball bearing, rolling and lubricated with reminiscence,
it is your uncle, the one who seems to have been old always.
As Lon Chaney, it remembers a good 700 faces.

With patience it can be taught to perform,
to jump and jab like a cupped bird, like the heart
of a cupped bird.

It doesn't really groan, maybe wheeze a little.
It can be flexed and make rifle sounds and go bald,
then withdraw, lie stiff and straight,

with a forlorn tremor of its thick walnut eyelid
on which reside the worry wrinkles
of the best minds of its generation.

Anti-Aubade

We sleep all morning and do not dream.
The sheets hold gently the filtered light.
Walls nod, standing. On the screen of our minds
Nothing is showing but white on white.
In the middle of a room in the middle
Of a house in the middle of our lives,
The alarm is off. The day is ours
To laze and doze, and have each other's halves.

Facing outward, our bodies just touching,
We make a fleshblot butterfly, saddle
Without rider or horse, breathing so calm
We might almost be dead, done with desires,
But for the imperceptible nudging,
The sweet, lingering kiss of our behinds.

You and I

for K. H.

You are the puzzle of shoelaces
and I am the bunny that goes through the hole.
I am a pair of lost glasses
and you are the top of my head.

You are a paper cut
and I am the disproportionate pain.
I am the flu-like symptoms
and you are the plenty of fluids.

You are the shopping list
and I am the milk it says not to get.
I am years of poor penmanship
and you are posthumous fame.

You are the calendar of Monets
and I am the dentist appointment next Friday at four.
I am filmy lenses
and you are the huff of breath.

You are the bedside radio
in the middle of the night
and I am the financial advice
that falls on your sleeping ears.

I am the familiar word
that just now looks unaccountably strange
and you are the spelling
that was correct all along.

Whenever I See Her

I am my father's son, I am John Donne
Whenever I see her with nothing on.
                    —Theodore Roethke, *The Swan*

Whenever I see her with nothing on
John Donne is just about the last person

anyone would be inclined to compare
me with, my father not least. To be sure,

I have my metaphysical moments
like everyone else, but she unpantsed,

the History of Ideas recedes
to airy thinness, several decades

of marriage notwithstanding. When I catch
a peek of her I half-suspect a glitch

in the universe, so unnatural
it seems, so anomalously surreal,

as though my eyes were seventeen again,
brimmed with all the guilty vistas heaven

obscures. In the movies, when the camera
lingers on the sequence of socks and bra,

slacks and blouse and tie, discreetly stopping
at the bed's edge—we discover peeping

is denied to us. So when now—Hurrah—
I finally get to pan the camera

up, it's like I am riding a jet ski
with her and my father and Ted Roethke.

Letter to My Penis

Dear Marcel,

Yesterday you were with me all day,
like a second head.
(You were the one with the beret.)

We strolled along the Seine, a couple
of cosmopolitans,
so Left Bankish, so très très chic.

We sat in the outdoor café with the blue
striped awnings.
An accordion came out of nowhere.

You crooned,
"Every little breeze seems to whisper chemise,"
and my blood purred.

I sipped espresso from a demitasse.
You buoyed your
cigarette holder with such savoir-faire,

such joie de vivre, I felt like taking you
by the shoulders
and giving you a peck on each cheek.

†

Who am I kidding? You know
we never did
any of that. Shameless, we got

sloshed on a bench in the Tenderloin,
savoring the butts
we'd scraped from the street.

Black bags hung from our
shopping cart.
Joggers adjusted their gaits.

We split a ketchup sandwich.
You peed in the alley.
I put on a dog collar and barked

at the pigeons
and watched them run. Such
was our fun.

†

My fickle paddle,
I tell you now:
You have rowed me in circles

long enough. Long enough,
Mr. Mopey Pinocchio,
have you sat in my lap, vacillating:

now the puppet, now the master,
now the tortured
artist, moody, brooding;

now the traffic sentinel,
officious on your podium with your pith helmet
and whistle and white gloves.

†

Coward that I am, I write
because I cannot say these things
to your face.

I know: The penis, like the heart,
has its reasons. And so
we may come to an understanding yet.

Mon frère, let's meet
tomorrow by the *Arc de Triomphe*.
I'll bring a box lunch.

We'll talk.

IV

Pinkie

here's my pinkie finger
weakest of any
I use it
for entering small places
nose holes eye nooks ear mazes

incorrigible pansy
scrupulous peon
immaculate pal o'mine

always at the end of things
like an aisle seat
always coy always
the lilting one
junior partner of the firm
the one who attends to the details
itself a detail
daughter I must leave out
of the Boy Scout salute
who flirts with my thumb
when I'm nervous

definitive unit of etiquette
meticulous imp
ultimate runt

I've tried to teach it guitar
make it type
play golf
karate
it's useless!
it wants to be insignificant or nothing
to know at the end no one
have no one

know it
unfamous as a thread
ninny of my care
stick without width

Thumb

To you, my bludgeon, comes the width
of years, the wiles, the bully's glance.
Blunt as you are, my first friend
and nourishment, you are

no bulwark of simplicity, no mug
merely, or underling, as you lumber
through night's sad mitten, fronting time,
plumped in your loneliness as in a psalm.

Dear squat padlock, I would not wrest from you
the fist, or stave off your brawn
to bluster with gentleness
the high-stacked anvils of grief.
I would not forge you into a kiss.

Old grappler, butt. How you must hate
the pinky, that cringing sissy,
all those mealy fingers
banding together against you.

Oppose them! My kickstand, my pug-
nacious übermensch.
In the brunt of dawn shall you rise
from your basement, weeping
and ruthless.

Index

This.
Is I. Is You. The One. The Only. First-born. Numero uno.
Identity.
That of course is They. The Many. The Rest. Cast
and chorus to this triumphant, starring
solo. Supreme,

it sweeps its wand of names over the world
and its lists.
Like any hero, it knows
no ambiguity, no shy yearning, no subterranean shame.
Not like that disgruntled schlub grumbling
off to the side. Not like
that crybaby at the other end,
sniffing back the tears of a scraped
knuckle. Nor that dad lording it over.
Nor that clinging
mom balancing the tableau. Rather, we have

this rugged digit of choice. The one you hold
forth with. The one that commands
attention. The one you count on
when you finally decide to
push the button, flip the switch, squeeze the trigger.

Starting quarterback. Squadron leader.
                              Peninsula of sanity
above the dribbling, wriggling mob.
Mast that holds together the rigging of your life.
Sturdy, certain axis. Protagonist you.
Honcho.
Integrity's own *J'accuse.*

Everyone knows the gun-in-the-trench-coat-pocket trick.
But think: What other would you trust to
gauge the wind
or wag a warning,
scour frosting
or trace a heart in the sand,
beckon a lover
or touch your nose
to show you're sober,
traverse a list
or pull out your cheek
to make a pop?

Who else would you have keep your place
in a book
or point the way
out of the jungle of things in which you are forever
getting lost?

Tall Man

"Fuck you!"
is all people seem to think I'm good for,
as though evolution had saved
this one
putting-assholes-in-their-places niche
just for me,
as though a jeer
were all I were or could ever be.

No Solomon
in truth was ever more solemn,
no monastery more stern
than this office of informing one's lessers
of their shortcomings,
of the manifold ways they fail,
invariably,
to measure up.

Think Abraham
Lincoln
as played by Raymond Massey,
or Michael Rennie as the noble alien
in *The Day the Earth Stood Still*,
come to convey
his grim admonition to humankind
to shape up or else.

Think Gregory Peck
in *To Kill a Mockingbird*.
(No one in the theater could ever be this good.)
Think Henry Fonda in *The Grapes of Wrath*
or *12 Angry Men* or *Fail-Safe*
or who knows how
many pictures

he loped his lanky decency
through.

I am of the tribe of these gaunt, leading men.
Sentinel and steeple, promontory
and lighthouse, monolith
and obelisk.
Robed pinnacle presiding
over the Sanhedrin of the fingers.
Bedouin patriarch. Pontiff. The one true north
off which everything
slopes, to which everything aspires
and falls short.

Some days
I wonder how anyone can stand
to be themselves.
From this sad height
I look down on them all,
parading around on the esplanade
of the palm,
tricked out in the only torsos
they'll ever know.

The scrawny snivelers cowering
across from the bowling ball bodies
of the bullies and blowhards;
the mesomorphs,
jocks without an ounce on them
of the fat of self-doubt,
unable to comprehend the flat-assed also-rans,
clinging and fawning.
                    And look:
there's me, too.
Self-appointed, towering tulip of rectitude!

Aloft. Aloof.
Candle. Javelin. Dad
frowning over your shoulder
all your life.

Thin bone of flame
rising.

A Plate of Scrambled Eggs

Attila Me surveys
the battlefield's pastel
upholstery from here
on high, and salivates,
imagining how grand,
how glorious to slash
the spineless masses through.
Take that! And that! You shreds!
You mangled carcasses,
you bundled, beaten goo.

The once exquisite yolks
are rumpled luggage now,
spreadeagled spongy flesh
I pummel with my tongue,
the battered yellow pads
like mud squished from a fist.
The cushion of a throat
submits like this, or would
were Jack the Ripper Me
arisen from the mist.

A good thing he's not. Else
these docile clouds defiled
with ravishment might well
belie the dignity
of that One True God: Me,
who sharpens even yet
his appetite among
the bright utensils
in the quiet kitchenette.

Stomach

Permanently punched is how it feels
today, like a bruised banana
or a rug being beaten
with a beater or run over
with a vacuum, bag bloated
with its mush of dust,
lint smoke chuffing out
at the least press.

In the end it's not the heart
to which the passions adhere,
but this baser tub, this inner sky,
across whose dark concavity
Dread, Rage, Shame, etc.
play their ferment out,
like aurora borealis
minus the awe.

Today the sun is a lump,
down here in here,
smudged above this rotunda
of walking wounded,
sunken death, tarred armies dug in
in the trenches and the murk,
the tender firmament
curving overhead.

In time one comes
to put by
the dent of everyday,
to deaden
the deaden-ness,
to slog on,
doubled over
even while standing straight.

On Taking Criticism

Noooooo! Not that line. Not that one.
How could anyone not be moved?
The way the short *i*'s glitter in the image
of the fin, the way the first word turns

savagely on the beauty of the last.
Like that dance routine where the French
sailor in the striped T-shirt and the brute
with the bandana around his neck jerk

the pleading blonde around, slapping her
to the barroom floor and yanking her back for more
abuse, until a knife appears and I forget
who gets it, but in any case the allusion to the fin

was ironic. I-ron-ic! Who could not see that?
Not appreciate the brave cliché,
the clever reveille of the *l*'s in *parallel*?
See how the break breaks

precisely three-fourths through, the way
the parentheses cup their hands around the ends
(calling out like Heidi's grandfather in the Alps,
or George trying to find Lennie before the others do.)

And at the end: that toothpick prick of realization,
the frisson as figure and ground leap through each other
like puzzle rings impossibly parted, everything
put to rights and the audience oohs, *Woooow*!

Who could not know? I might as well revise
my being as that line that is all
that I am. Anyone would be crazy
not to love it as I do.

The Formalist Flattered

for R. F.

"Unlike some poets," my friend tells me,
"you don't barf on the page."
Sweet of her to say so, sweet that she
might think to disengage
me from the lax, ill-mannered hordes
with their prolific barf,
those for whom every word's
a kind of holy *Arf.*

But while it's true my notebook
may betray a penchant for the proper,
gussied forms over which I futz,
I do sometimes spit up a speck,
an eyedropper
of my guts.

The Plagiarizer of Words

Out of the streaming radio of voices in the café,
out of the sports section spread before him
on the tiny round table they stick you with at Peet's,
out of Dunn's *New and Selected Poems 1974-1994*
obscuring the scores, not to mention
the junk drawer in the dresser of his head,

he snitches words like a frog snatching flies:
    thimble haphazard numbskull
which collage themselves like Rockettes which
sets him off on:
    collision kalashnikov
the syllables wiggling and kicking in his mouth
next to the hazelnut muffin.

Before long he finds himself ventriloquizing
(so as not to seem too crazy to those around):
    garaggge zzzhivago jjje ne sais quoi
his coffeed head now kazooing like a dozen bees
which in turn brings him back to: *numbskull.*

The air is reverent with fraudulence, fraudulent
with reverie! He loves splashing about in language,
bucket in hand, toeing the debris.
From Dunn this morning he pockets:
    jetty pucker obstinate

Flipping back then to the live program around him:
    fidget swivel potluck
He thinks what a stew it all is, and how plucky his Bubby,
a girl back in Romania peeling turnips, wiping her hands
on a coarse brown apron. Then strolling out,
smuggled under his breath:
    babushka babussshka ba-busssssh-ka

Umlaut

(After *O, pardon me, thou bleeding piece of earth*)

O, dimpled debris, you foreign peas of little girth,
So sleek and fragile above these slackers,
Timbered colon on the tide of lines,
What art you make of the ponderest thought.
Kudos to the scribe that sudsed you up!
Over these runes how you do ululate,
Never mind their slatted feet and fingery pews
And tupled riffs that taffy up the tongue,
Your freckles froth forth above the thrum of them.
Speckled, spackled, owling vowels' brows,
Your confettied jetsam so petite,
And trinkets and eyelets so enskyed,
That poets may pee in their pants to see
Your spangles sprinkled on their piles of snore,
All gravity whisked from the dull feeds.
Now your drizzled pixels surging from the sludge,
With caret and tilde at their side,
Seem with a vaulter's arch to kick up
Out of the page. And though we cry *Come back!*
Come back! you renounce this broth of logs,
That your fled motes might dwell above the earth
Like caroming stars crooning and burstable.

&

Ampersand: Contraction of *and per se and*.... The symbol
comes from an old Roman system of shorthand signs
(*ligatures*), attested in Pompeian graffiti.

(After *Tomorrow and tomorrow and tomorrow*)

And per se and per se and per se,
sweeps in this alluring ligature to the last pretzel
of corrugated might. Who knew

the graffiti in Pompeii would come down to this
jocular flourish, this whirly thingamabob
flaunting the apostrophe of its pompadour?

The equation of its curve looks like sinuses
feel when spring's springs spring into them.
Foolish and elegant. Busty death behind.

Mae West with a bow tie and a menu,
a shallow bowl of soup pronged in the trivet
of her short hand. Here, here, bulbous epithet!

Life's but a hectic filigree, all hairpin and no straightaway;
the loopy smoke of a knuckle ball; a thumbprint
wrapped in a mandala in a dolma in the Magna Carta;

a randy, pampered ampere teased into a rococo
coxcomb that goes fritzing and futzing, "Et tu, Et?"
and "Tag, you're it.", its floral upon the page.

What does it all mean?

It is a tangle tied to a dendrite,
furled, untoward and horny,
amplifying doodly-squat.

Two Saints of Clarity

During the invasion of Syracuse,
or so the story goes, Archimedes
was sitting in the road engrossed
with a problem he'd scratched into the dust,
and pleaded with the centurion
who'd swaggered up, hot to run
him through, to be spared a brief
minute only, to scribble out the proof.

Antoine Lavoisier, so it is said,
the night before he was to be beheaded
took tea and attended to his hair,
having arranged with the executioner
to hold the still-thinking thing up to the crowd,
that his confederate, the celebrated
mathematician Lagrange, might count his blinks,
and so settle a fine point of science.

So what if the story-tellers lied?
Reason loves its legends too, fables that
inflame, like the tales of these saints
of clarity, on whose dying faces
appeared no rouge of adoration or
piety, transfiguration or prayer—
just pure curiosity, peering out,
unperturbed, above the rushing blood.

Long Division

Griefs
go
into
grief.

Someday
all
will
die

and
grieving
end,
leaving

zero
sorrow.

We Here

Ring,
gravestone
phone,
ring!

Grace
our
outer
office.

We
here
hear
the
marble
warble.

Graph Paper

Once the truth was gooey thunder. A wad
of spirits glommed on every tree and rock.
Rainbows gauzed their signatures. Green wonder
knelt before the omens. Rapt, agog. Me,

I love these acred cubbyholes, the lace
they leave on sea and sky, on stone, on bush;
this wickerwork of our Cartesian souls,
these lucid rooms and numbered pairs. This skin.

Keep your smug romantics who idolize
the blur, the smudge, the gush, the night. Give me
this plane of sanity where blue semantics
rules the earth, and every angle is right.

The Mark of Zorro

Ha! I cry and swish
   my trademark Z, laughing as
the world's pants fall down

About the Author

Roy Mash produces his quota of carbon dioxide in Marin County, California, doodling his brief time away staring out of café windows, dabbing up the seeds that have fallen from an everything bagel, anticipating the arrival of The Mummy making his inexorable way across the globe on his mission to ~~Detroit~~ San Rafael.

Below, the artist has caught the author's likeness with uncanny accuracy.

CPSIA information can be obtained at www.ICGtesting.com
Printed in the USA
BVOW02s1016181113

336507BV00001B/7/P